CA$H IN ON
YOUR SKILLS

WAYS TO
MAKE MONEY
WITH ART

ANGIE TIMMONS

Enslow Publishing
101 W. 23rd Street
Suite 240
New York, NY 10011
USA

enslow.com

Published in 2020 by Enslow Publishing, LLC.
101 W. 23rd Street, Suite 240, New York, NY 10011

Cataloging-in-Publication Data

Names: Timmons, Angie.
Title: Ways to make money with art / Angie Timmons.
Description: New York : Enslow Publishing, 2020. | Series: Cash in on your skills | Includes glossary and index.
Identifiers: ISBN 9781978515420 (pbk.) | ISBN 9781978515437 (library bound)
Subjects: LCSH: Money-making projects for children--Juvenile literature.Art--Vocational guidance--Juvenile literature.
Classification: LCC HF5381.2 T56 2020 | DDC 331.702--dc23

Printed in China

To Our Readers: We have done our best to make sure all websites in this book were active and appropriate when we went to press. However, the author and the publisher have no control over and assume no liability for the material available on those websites or on any websites they may link to. Any comments or suggestions can be sent by email to customerservice@enslow.com.

Portions of this book originally appeared in *Money-Making Opportunities for Teens Who Are Artistic* by Gina Hagler.

Photo Credits: Cover Di Studio/Shutterstock.com; p. 5 © iStockphoto.com/Steve Debenport; p. 6 Jeff Greenberg/Photolibrary/Getty Images; p. 9 RossHelen/iStock/Getty Images; p. 12 milindri/iStock/Getty Images; p. 15 Casimiro PT/Shutterstock.com; p. 17 Iakov Filimonov/Shutterstock.com; pp. 21, 63 sturti/E+/Getty Images; p. 23 RosaIreneBetancourt 7/Alamy Stock Photo; p. 25 Ableimages/DigitalVision/Getty Images; p. 27 fstop123/iStock/Getty Images; p. 31 fizkes/iStock/Getty Images; p. 34 Hill Street Studios/DigitalVision/Getty Images; p. 36 © iStockphoto.com/FatCamera; pp. 38, 52 Rawpixel.com/Shutterstock.com; p. 41 Imgorthand/E+/Getty Images; p. 44 Wavebreakmedia/iStock/Getty Images; p. 48 GaudiLab/Shutterstock.com; p. 51 Doug Menuez/Forrester Images/Photodisc/Getty Images; p. 56 Peter Dazeley/Photographer's Choice/Getty Images; p. 59 Ljupco Smokovski/Shutterstock.com; p. 61 Dean Drobot/Shutterstock.com; p. 65 Jim West/Alamy Stock Photo; p. 67 monkeybusinessimages/iStock/Getty Images.

CONTENTS

When Moziah "Mo" Bridges was nine years old, he couldn't find a bowtie to complete the fashionable look he was going for. He had a vision for his personal style, and no bowtie could satisfy that vision.

Taught by his grandmother to cut and sew fabric, the stylish young man from Memphis decided to create his own bowtie. With help from his grandmother, he began producing more ties and selling them in markets. He soon had a business going: Mo's Bows. Within a year, his business was featured in several magazines. Within a couple of years, he was invited to appear on *The Steve Harvey Show* and the ABC entrepreneurial-themed reality show *Shark Tank*.

At just eleven years old, Mo didn't even know what *Shark Tank* was when he was invited to appear on the show. Some friends told him it was a popular show where entrepreneurs present their business ideas to a panel of investors to try to get funding. The show's panel offered to invest in Mo's Bows when Mo (with help from his mother and business manager, Tramica Morris) made his presentation, but young Mo declined their offer to instead receive

At just nine years old, Moziah Bridges started on his path to success by using his artistic vision to design his own bowtie business and cash in on his skills.

free mentorship from one of the panelists, businessman Daymond John, who had started a clothing line (For Us By Us, or "FUBU") as a young man.

Mo continued to get attention and make appearances on national television shows as he grew his tie business. In 2015, at just thirteen years old, he made *Time* magazine's 30 Most Influential Teens List. He made the list again in 2017—the same year he signed a lucrative partnership deal with the National Basketball Association (NBA) allowing Mo to use NBA logos on his products and for sales purposes. By 2018, the sixteen-year-old was making six figures with his tie company, was giving to multiple charities, had been invited to the White House, and was keeping his eye on the prize. He told the *Memphis Business Journal*

If you're artistic and want to turn your creativity into a profitable business, pursue it! There are many ways to get experience and develop a business—even at a young age.

Journal in January 2018 "he wanted to become a fashion designer and design for pop culture's biggest influencers."

In the span of seven years, a little boy who started out with the simple goal of making his own bowtie created a profitable, headline-worthy business empire.

There are many other ways to put creative and

own opportunities through entrepreneurship like Mo did. But don't underestimate the traditional jobs connected to artistic interests as well as internship and volunteer opportunities that could be the first step to the career of your dreams!

Get Creative: Think About Entrepreneurship

You've looked at your available options to make money as a young person: babysitting, mowing lawns, tutoring, dog walking, and the occasional odd job for someone in the neighborhood. None of them are your thing, but you're either too young for other jobs or you're not interested in the ones you can get—like checking groceries or working at a fast food restaurant. Regardless, you need to make money.

Fortunately, you're artistic. You can draw and paint. You can sculpt and create mosaics. You can make jewelry and other accessories or sew. In fact, there are many things you can think of to create with your hands and some artistic supplies. Plus, doing projects that use your artistic talents is a lot of fun. Someday, you plan to work in an art-related field, such as graphic design or computer animation or fashion. So, what's keeping you from putting your artistic talents to work right now? Believe it or not,

Using your artistic talents is not only fun but could be a way to set yourself apart from others and make money. You just need to find your unique place in the artistic market.

you can get paid for doing what you love while you are still a teenager.

Find Your Creative Place

The first step is finding your niche—the place in the market that only you can occupy. Maybe your original anime characters are huge favorites with your friends. Maybe everyone who sees the mural you've drawn on your bedroom wall falls in love with it. Maybe your latest jewelry or self-made fashion item draws admirers every time. Whatever it is that sets you apart from the crowd is just the thing to make your own opportunity.

There is a trick to finding a good niche. It needs to be specific enough that people can appreciate the uniqueness of what you do, yet broad enough that a lot of people will consider your services. While you are trying to find your niche, take some time to think about the things you love to create. Then think about the reactions your friends and others have to your creations. Chances are good that if they are excited about your work, paying customers will be, too. Get some of your friends to brainstorm with you. No idea is too crazy. Encourage people to tell you what they like most or what they would like to see you create. At the end of the brainstorming session, you'll have a list of ideas to explore.

Suppose everyone agrees that your fashion items are terrific. A quick search shows that lots of people do fashion design. What sets you apart from those other designers? Do you want to be known as the person who does fashion for children? How about the person who does fashion for adults? Maybe you can see yourself creating fashion for all age groups and for all kinds of people.

Let's say you are drawn to the idea of creating fashion for children. Maybe you'll decide your niche is making fashionable clothing for children, like Mo Bridges set out to do for himself as a nine-year-old. Spend some time drawing fashion items and see what you come up with. If you like creating shirts and accessories, include some children might like. For instance, do the children you know love a certain color? A particular accessory? Create some samples. Use bright colors and images to bring your design ideas to life.

Maybe you are crazy about anime. You love to create characters and make up stories about them. Perhaps your niche is making graphic novels that feature your characters. You could create handmade books to sell on the comics market. Or, you might create large inked drawings of your anime characters in action, suitable for framing and hanging. It's up to you to define your niche. Once you do, you will be known as the person who creates that type of art.

Show Off

Once you've decided upon your niche, it's time to do some networking and see if your idea might meet the needs of paying customers.

First, you'll need to gather polished samples of your work that you can show potential clients. For example, if your niche is doing fashion items, consider offering free samples in exchange for photographs of people wearing your creations and references from the client. Make sketches of other fashionable items you could create for clients. Include some drawings you think boys would like, some that girls would like, some that are not gender-specific, and some that are

Always keep up with samples of your work. Compile them in a professional portfolio so you can show your artistic ability to potential customers and employers.

for very young children. If you are open to a variety of styles, include several styles in your samples. Put all your samples in a binder or portfolio case. Make sure this collection is easy for potential clients to browse.

Perhaps graphic art is your niche, and you are interested in designing logos for small businesses. There are many sources for small business owners to order customized business cards, stationery, and other materials using premade formats and graphics. However, most would prefer to have something that is unique. Gather some samples of your work, perhaps designs you created for friends or relatives, and then approach some small businesses with them. If you're not sure how to find small business owners, see if your local chamber of commerce or small business center can help you.

The Online Potential

Instead of providing art-related services, maybe you can create unique craft items to sell on the internet. You may be talented at making decorated clothing, personalized baby gifts, or custom models, just to name a few. Some artistic teens start their own online stores or participate in existing online stores, such as Etsy.com, to sell this type of merchandise.

BUSINESS BASICS

For an idea to succeed as a business, it has to offer a product that people want. Additionally, the entrepreneur needs to be able to provide that product at a reasonable cost and turn a profit. For instance, your idea might be to create a clothing line for triplets. Is that a viable business? How many triplets are born each month in your town? The answer is likely not very many. But, if you know of a group for parents of triplets, you might be able to market to them directly and make sales.

By defining your niche, identifying potential customers, and considering the costs, you'll determine if your idea would make a successful business. Remember, the goal is to use your artistic and creative talents to create something of value to a steady stream of potential customers. Without customers, your idea can't become a business.

Embellished, or decorated, clothing can include a vast array of items, from painted or ribbon-adorned T-shirts to stenciled sneakers and bejeweled jeans. If you're not sure what will sell, you can create samples to put on a website. You'll quickly see what sells and what doesn't.

If you are good at making custom models, check out what's selling at the local hobby shop. While some people like creating models themselves, someone who is creating an entire fleet or army might welcome the chance to have some of the work done for him.

Baby items are always in demand. Painted blocks or signs made with non-toxic, baby safe paint are popular, as are onesies with funny sayings on them and handmade headbands for little girls.

Whatever product you choose, make sure there

Online stores like Etsy are great ways for young entrepreneurs to sell their creative wares. Artists can set up their own online shops and sell directly to customers.

is something about it that makes it unique. Creating an online store may sound complicated, but it doesn't have to be. You can set up your store using a free blogging application. Your products can be displayed as images and descriptions within blog posts. You can categorize your posts and then use the categories as the menu items on the blog. Customers can then click on T-shirts, for example, and see all the different designs you have for sale. To place an order, customers can contact you through a form on the site or at an e-mail address you create for your business. To accept payment, you can establish a merchant account with companies like PayPal.

Kids and Creativity

Some artistic teens who enjoy working with kids decide to combine their artistic talents with child-care services to create their niche. For example, they may provide an art activity with each babysitting assignment. Some of the projects may take more than one babysitting visit to complete. Others can be completed in one night or afternoon. These teens can charge more than a typical babysitter because they offer additional value. Also, they're likely to be in higher demand. Parents are happy because their kids are doing something creative. Kids are happy because they have something fun to do. To give

Teaching art to children is one way for young entrepreneurs to make money. Advertise as a babysitter who teaches art or start a class geared toward children interested in art.

parents an idea of what types of projects you can do with their children, make several project boxes. In each box, include the materials that you will use in the activity and a finished sample.

Summer activities, school-break camps, and group babysitting on weekends are additional services you can offer parents. Offer your services for several hours as an art camp or workshop. The children can choose from a variety of projects. If the camp is ongoing, pick a different theme each week.

Have the campers create a variety of items based on that theme. At the end of the week, invite the parents to an art show with the completed work on display. Once again, samples of the types of projects you offer will be an important part of your marketing efforts. If some of the projects are large or complicated, include a photo of a finished project or a description of what the project will entail.

Birthday parties are another great opportunity for artistic and entrepreneurial teens. You can lead the guests in doing a craft project at the party. Or, you can offer your services to create custom party favors and decorations. Customers can have the best of both worlds if you lead the children in creating their own party favors. The party will be special because of the art activity you provide. The favors will be special because the kids created them. As part of your marketing, present samples of the favors guests can create. People will want to see examples of your ideas before they decide to hire you for their child's party.

Once you decide upon a niche that will support a business, you are on your way to becoming an entrepreneur. Remember that opportunities are all around you. The important thing is the ability to recognize and seize these opportunities.

Go Traditional with Your Creativity

Not all creative young people are prepared to start a business and share it with the world like Mo Bridges. Most of us need a path that offers a little more guidance to hone our skills, get experience, and get paid. That might mean a traditional job with an existing business that's willing to employ you for your creative skills. This may be especially appealing to people who would like to get some real-world experience that also offers set work hours and pay. Finding these kinds of opportunities will vary depending on your age, skill set, and how much competition there is for the position.

Tips for Success

A positive attitude is the most important thing you'll need when looking for a job that uses your artistic abilities. You are going to meet a lot of people in your search for a job. Some of the people will be in a position to help you. Others may not. All of them will form an impression of you—so make it a good one! Since you'll be looking for jobs that use your talents many times over the years, here are some tips for successful networking and job searching:

- Dress appropriately when looking for a job. This is not the time for cutoff jeans and a ratty T-shirt. Wear something you feel comfortable in, but make sure it is nicer than what you wear to at school or to go out to the movies with your friends.
- Bring a business card with you. It should have your name, email address, and phone number. You can buy blank business cards and create and print your own. You can also use an online service to create and print your own design.
- Make eye contact with the person you're speaking to. Offer your hand for a handshake when you first meet. Introduce yourself. Explain that you're looking for a job that will use your artistic talents.
- Turn your phone off and leave it in your bag or pocket.
- Think ahead about what you'll say about yourself and your experience. It's helpful to prepare a short pitch that describes the top

If you have the opportunity to use your artistic skills in a professional, traditional environment, present yourself in a professional manner to make a good impression.

skills you have to offer. Practice it in front of the mirror.

- Bring samples of your work in a notebook or portfolio.
- Bring a pen in case you need to complete an application. Ask your neighbors or teachers ahead of time if you can use them as references. If they say yes, ask them for a telephone number you can include on the application.

Even if someone does not have a job for you right now, leaving your contacts with a positive impression of you is important. Then when they do have an appropriate opportunity—or learn of an opening that someone else wants to fill—you will be high on the list of candidates.

Who Could Use Your Skills?

Think about the kinds of organizations that might need a person with artistic abilities. You'll be surprised at how many businesses and nonprofits can use your skills. The opportunities range from the after-school program at a local elementary school to the weekly programs held at your local arts or community center. Many religious schools also include art in their weekly education programs. Ask your friends and relatives about the programs they participate in, or the programs they participated in when they were younger, as a way of learning about local programs that include art. You can also browse directories of community resources online, such as on your local Patch site.

Think After School

After-school programs are good places for artistic

teens to look for jobs. Some of these programs focus specifically on art. Instructors can often use an assistant to prepare and distribute supplies or to work with small groups of children within the larger group.

To find out where art programs are held after school, check the website of your local school or school district. The PTA (Parent-Teacher Association) section may be especially helpful. It may offer flyers or details for the programs. If there are no art after-school programs available, maybe

After-school programs at places like community centers or through religious organizations are great places to do good with your artistic skills.

there is a general after-school program that could use your talents. Such programs usually include art in their activities.

Call the program's director or organizer and ask if you can stop by and introduce yourself. Think about what you want to say beforehand. Practice a few times before you make the call. Make some notes that you can refer to as you speak. Then relax and pretend you're speaking to the parent of a friend. If the director agrees to meet with you, be prepared. For an art program, bring a sample of your work. For a general after-school program, bring a sample and some ideas for the projects you would do with the children.

Local Arts Centers

You can also consider applying for a job at a nonprofit arts center. Local and regional arts centers usually provide a number of arts opportunities in the form of classes or camps. Some of these programs are for children and others are for adults. On weekends and holidays, there may also be parent-child classes. Any of these classes might need an assistant.

Check the center's schedule and see which programs fit with your talents. For example, many arts centers have a darkroom that could use teens with experience in photography. They are sure to have drawing and painting classes. Pottery classes,

Classes at after-school programs, local and regional arts centers, community centers, and nonprofits may offer paid teaching opportunities for young artists and creatives.

in which students throw their own pots before glazing them, are another common offering at an arts center. Sculpture is often offered, too. Prepare some samples of your work and arrange a time to stop by to introduce yourself.

Community and Recreation Centers

Even if your town or city doesn't have an arts

LABOR LAWS

The Fair Labor Standards Act (FLSA) protects children from working in unsafe conditions and from working too much to receive adequate education or rest.

Federal labor law varies by age for teens in terms of what kind of work they can do and how many hours they can work. The good news for artistic teens is that federal labor regulations list "work of an intellectual or artistically creative nature" as work that is not prohibited for younger teens (fourteen- and fifteen-year-olds). However, still check the provisions of your state's child labor laws for the description of work of an artistically creative nature, the age at which teens are eligible for that work, the number of hours and times of day that you can work, pay rates, and whether you'll need any working papers or permits. Ask your school's guidance counselor for help.

center, it may have a community or recreation center. Community centers are usually funded and run by the city, by a nonprofit agency, or by a religious organization. In addition to programs for youth, many of these centers offer programs for the elderly. There may even be a senior center in your community. If you like spending time communicating with and helping older people, this may be a great option for you. Check out your local community or senior center and see what programs are offered. Then think of some projects that might work for this age group before putting together samples of your work and stopping by.

Recreation centers and city or countywide recreation programs are likely to offer art and craft classes for a variety of ages. Again, check what is being offered, match it with your abilities and interests, and apply for a job. With your talent and

Teaching art doesn't have to be limited to children—senior centers or agencies with senior programs may be looking for talented artists to teach art programs.

enthusiasm for art, you will be an excellent addition.

Religious Options

Religious schools are schools run by churches, synagogues, and other houses of worship to provide education about religion. Many religious schools have classes after school or on weekends that include art projects. Those near you might need some help. Check the website for the religious institution. Try to locate the name of the principal of the school, as well as the name of the art teacher, if the school has one. These individuals may have phone numbers or email addresses listed. Try to arrange a time to stop by and meet one or both of these people. As with your other applications, be sure to provide samples of your work and some information about why you would be an excellent person for the job.

Look the Part

The way you present yourself makes a difference in whether or not you are offered a job. A positive attitude and appropriate dress help you make a good first impression. It's also important to showcase your qualifications for the job. Your portfolio, résumé, and work samples are essential to this effort. Bringing these materials demonstrates that you are serious about the opportunity. Remember that anything you bring must be in a form that reflects well on you. Take the time to proofread your materials and display them in a neat and organized fashion.

Say It All in Your Portfolio

As an artist, your portfolio is your calling card. It is an introduction to who you are as an artist. Because of this, it's essential that the work you choose for your portfolio is work you are proud of. To increase your chances of landing a job, it's a good idea to include work in more than one genre. For instance, if you are a photographer, bring along prints that illustrate the kind of work you do. It might be black-and-white work that you developed yourself or digital work that you edited with photo-editing software. If you also sketch or paint, bring along work that represents your abilities in that genre. If you make mosaics, pottery, stained glass, or sculpture, you can include some of those pieces in your portfolio as well. It doesn't make sense to lug around larger creations, but including images that show the intricacies of your work will be just right.

If you can afford one, purchase a portfolio case at an art supply store. There are many different types. Pick the one that is the best size for your work. If a portfolio case is too expensive, buy some page protector sleeves and put your work in a binder. Be sure that your work is organized and neat.

Create Your Résumé

As a teen, you probably don't have a lot of professional experience to include on a résumé. But you do have classes you've taken, camps or special programs you've attended, and projects you've worked on. Put your name and contact information at the top of a typed page that includes this information. Break the information into categories, such as classes, summer programs, and projects. List the name and date of each program. Include a brief summary of the program or project in a line or two—just enough to give someone skimming the résumé a good idea of what you did. Explain what you accomplished during the course of the program. If you've received any awards or other forms of recognition, include them in a separate section at the bottom. Also include any special art programs you have participated in at school or outside school. The idea is to give the person reading your résumé a good idea of what you've accomplished in the art field.

Interviewing

You already know that making a good first impression is important. Making eye contact, offering to shake hands, introducing yourself, and speaking clearly—these are the minimum you'll need to do to get a job. To really win over the interviewer, you'll need to answer questions in a way that clearly connects your personal qualities, experiences, and artistic talents to the particular job being offered. You want to show the interviewer that you can meet the demands of the position and solve problems for him or her.

If you're asked why you are the ideal candidate, be sure to mention that you're a hard worker, you

It's never too early to create and build your résumé with the classes and programs you've taken and any job experience you already have.

learn quickly, you're eager for this opportunity, and you're excited to put your talents to work. Sincere enthusiasm and energy count for a lot. If you're asked about a past mistake, you can tell the interviewer what it was. Just be sure to include what you learned from the experience.

Show Your Work

If you are suggesting new projects or programs for an organization, it may be helpful to bring along a sample of the finished product you are suggesting. Maybe it will be a treasure box or a decorated journal. Whatever it is, pick something that will communicate your talents and your understanding of the goals of the program. If the project is large, a series of images may be more practical than a sample. Use your judgment. Remember, you're there to introduce yourself, make a positive impression, present some of your work, and explain why you're the perfect person to hire. Everything you tell and show the interviewer should help to make this case.

Other Ways to Get Experience

Not all of us are out to make a buck or start a business. Sure, making money and making a name for yourself sound great, but the conditions for those outcomes aren't always in place—maybe the economy isn't great right now, or maybe you're more interested in getting experience than getting paid. Internships and volunteer positions are great avenues to get experience, make connections, and build your portfolio. You might not get paid, but these opportunities can be invaluable for your future. You can also use your talents to do work you enjoy while taking steps toward the career you want. You'll rack up interesting experiences that will set your college applications and essays apart from others. The more committed you are to your volunteer work or internship, the more you'll gain from it.

Internships

An internship is an opportunity to work for a business or organization before you are old enough or have all the qualifications needed to be hired there. An internship may or may not be a paid position. People seek internships as a way of gaining experience in the field they hope to enter one day. Many different organizations offer internships that are of interest to teens with artistic talent.

Museums often have internship programs for those interested in careers as curators, museum educators, or other museum professionals. Artistic interns may also work on the exhibits in museums, aquariums, zoos, nature centers, and other public

Museums, theaters, art galleries, and other artistic venues may offer internships to enterprising teens who want to get some real-world experience.

places. They also may work on set design and props for live theater.

The community organizations near you may offer internships for artistic teens. One way to find out is to visit your school's guidance office and ask about internship opportunities. Another way is to ask your art teachers. You can also research organizations on your own. Check the websites of institutions where you'd like to work and see if they have any information about internships. Or call the organizations and ask to speak to a human resources hiring professional. That person should be able to tell you about the organization's internship opportunities or direct you to someone else who can. If all of that fails, try calling the department that does the type of work you are interested in, and see if you can arrange an internship that way.

Volunteering

Volunteering is a great way to gain experience. It is also a terrific way to learn to work with people. You'll have a supervisor, fellow volunteers, and people that you lead in art projects or do artistic work for. There are a lot of different possibilities, and each of them is an opportunity for you to develop valuable skills.

Serving as a volunteer is also a great way to become involved in your community. You'll meet

Using your artistic abilities to volunteer may not make you any money, but you'll do a lot of good by working with people who could use your help.

people you might never have known—dedicated people who are making a difference in your area. You'll work on worthy projects while using your artistic talents.

How do you find volunteer opportunities that are right for you? Checking with your guidance counselor is a great first step. Approaching organizations that do the type of work you're interested in is another way. The important thing is to keep your eyes open. Think about how you'd like to use your artistic talents. Then think about organizations or other places where this type of work is done. When you have a match, ask if there are volunteer opportunities. Chances are very good that a volunteer with your talents will be welcome.

School and Service Opportunities

Many schools have mandatory volunteer requirements for their students. If your school has this requirement, it is likely to have a list of organizations that are preapproved for student volunteers. Check to see whether any of these organizations are looking for teens with artistic ability. You may find there's a perfect fit between what you love to do and what an organization needs.

In addition, many schools offer student service learning (SSL) as an option for students or as a requirement for graduation. Student service learning is an education method that links academic learning with student service that benefits the community.

Both volunteering and service learning can provide opportunities for artistic teens to get valuable real-world experience. For example, many nonprofits have volunteer positions that use artistic

Volunteering can take many forms—you can work with needy people one-on-one or you can collaborate with other groups and other people to work on big artistic projects.

ability. You might design flyers for an upcoming event, help with a brochure that will be mailed to potential donors, or create art activities for children. Any of these projects can provide you with finished products for your portfolio. At the same time, you'll have the chance to help a nonprofit that wouldn't otherwise have access to someone with your talent.

Community and Youth Groups

Your community may have volunteer organizations that bring meals to the homebound elderly or provide babysitting for working mothers. It's likely one of these organizations could use the services of a teen with artistic ability. You might design posters that publicize the group's work or greeting cards the organization could use to raise funds. You might create coloring pages to entertain children. Taking the time to learn about volunteer organizations in your community is a great way to discover a place for you and your talents.

Youth groups, such as 4-H and scouting, offer programs and merit badges in the arts. For instance, 4-H offers an entire curriculum for those who are interested in the visual art of photography. The Boy Scouts of America offers merit badges in basketry, drafting, graphic arts, landscape architecture, leatherwork, model design and building, painting, photography, and pottery to name a few. Similarly, there are plenty of art opportunities for girls through the Girl Scouts of the USA. For instance, there are merit badges in woodworking, book art, digital movie making, and comic art. Any of these programs provide an opportunity for you to learn more about an area of art that interests you.

EXTRACURRICULARS

You don't always have to look outside your immediate surroundings for opportunities. Many schools offer clubs, classes, and extracurriculars that can offer you the opportunity to express your talent and grow your creativity. If your school doesn't offer a club specific to your skill (like an art club), then start one. If you want to go bigger, volunteer to work on the creative needs of your school's next theater production. That could include music, lighting, set design, costumes, and any number of creative and artistic needs. Don't look at art as something that will be a big part of your life one day. Find a way to make what you love a part of your daily life right now.

Get Good While Doing Good

Another way to approach volunteer opportunities is to think of the skills you'd like to have for the future. Which skills are important for your college application? Which skills are essential to your future job prospects? Once you've identified these skills, you'll be in a better position to find a volunteer position or internship that will give you the chance to develop them.

Look for programs in your area that can help you get a head start in your artistic career, like classes at local community colleges or community centers that teach valuable artistic skills.

For example, you might dream of working in video game design in the future. With your artistic skills, you can create amazing characters in an elaborate setting. The local community college may offer a class in video game design that focuses on programming. Perhaps you could offer your artistic skills to the class. In exchange for designs that bring the visual part of the game to life, you could participate in the class and learn about the programming involved. Opportunities like this are worth exploring.

If ceramics is your thing, you could volunteer to help customers with more ambitious projects at the local ceramics store. Many towns have stores where people make and glaze their own pottery or decorate ready-made items. But many of the people who participate don't have a lot of art experience. There are a number of different ways to create special effects, but many customers don't know how to execute them. Your volunteer efforts would give you experience with these effects. It would also give you experience teaching and working with others.

Headed for Success

By the end of a summer or semester of volunteering or interning, you will have some serious experience, as well as evidence to help document your accomplishments. In addition, you will have many transferable skills that you can use in volunteer or paid positions in the future.

Tell Your Story

Your portfolio will definitely grow as a result of your volunteer work. You'll have pictures of your projects to include in your portfolio. If you worked with groups of adults or kids, include photos of yourself interacting with them if you can. It will give someone leafing through your portfolio the chance to fully understand your role and what you contributed as a volunteer.

If some of your artwork is elaborate or detailed, take photos that show those artistic touches. You can include close-up shots along with photos that show the work in its entirety. If your role was to teach others, you can show examples of your students' art to demonstrate the results of your instruction.

Remember, your portfolio tells the story of your work. Be sure your artistic talent and creativity speak for you.

People Skills

Employers and colleges want candidates who are self-motivated and able to work well independently. However, these qualities alone are not everything you'll need. The ability to work well with others has been important since your very first playgroup or preschool experience. You'll also need to show future employers and colleges that you work well with others.

As an adult professional, you'll often work on large projects that include a number of people. The

Volunteering and interning can provide you with valuable people skills and collaboration experience that colleges and future employers will value.

people may be from one group or department, or from several. If you have a reputation for being a good communicator or team player with a lot of talent, you will be an artist in demand.

Your volunteer and internship experiences provide you with several types of people skills.

The first is your ability to work with and for your supervisor. The second is your ability to cooperate with other staff or volunteers to get a job done. Another is your ability to relate to the individuals or groups you are serving. Having proven experience in these areas to include in your college application, résumé, or skills summary is important.

References: Think Ahead

In addition to learning new skills, working with others, and using your talents to help a worthy cause, volunteering or interning can also be a source of references. References are people who can attest to your strengths in letters of recommendation or in phone conversations with future employers.

It may be a while before you need a letter of recommendation that is geared toward a specific job or opportunity. However, it's a good idea to ask for a general letter of recommendation at the end of your time as a volunteer or intern, while your work is still fresh in your supervisor's mind. He or she can describe your responsibilities and the way you carried them out. Save the letter in your portfolio to show other potential employers someday.

Your references may also be in a position to tell you about other opportunities, now and in the future. Make sure you ask for some time to speak with your supervisors about what you hope to do with your artistic talents in the future. Thank them for the opportunity to work with and learn from them, and check in with them occasionally after you leave. If they are working in positions that use their own artistic talents, they'll certainly understand what it takes to get started. If you are talented and eager, and have done good work for them, it's likely they'll be happy to help you as you try to launch your career.

Starting Your Creative Business

Y ou've considered your options and decided you want to start your own business: creating custom ceramic pieces. You want to make personalized plates, baby sets, and special-purpose bowls and platters.

You feel good about your business's potential. There's just one major consideration: knowing how to create a great product and knowing how to run a business aren't exactly the same skill set. If you are going to be doing this on your own, you need to learn some basics about maintaining records and making a profit.

The Business Plan

A business plan is a good way to think through your idea from start to finish. You can use special software that helps you prepare a basic business plan. If you are starting a small, simple business, you can first prepare a plan that covers the most important aspects of a successful business. As you grow, you

If you want to be an artistic entrepreneur, you'll need a business plan that details what you'll be selling, how you plan to sell it, and an ownership structure.

can become more sophisticated in your planning. You can prepare a more exhaustive business plan before you expand or make a significantly large investment in your business.

Business Description

The first part of a business plan is a description of your business. What will the business do? Who will be doing it? Where will it be done? For the ceramics business, you might write that you will be creating ceramic pieces with custom designs. You will be the one doing the work. It will be done at the local ceramics store.

The description should include your form of business ownership. This refers to whether your business is a corporation, an LLC (Limited Liability Company), a partnership, or a sole proprietorship (also known as a Schedule C business). You can speak to a lawyer or tax accountant or read about the different types of businesses on the Internal Revenue Service (IRS) website (www.irs.gov) or in books to learn more.

Most likely you'll begin as a sole proprietor. This means that you and the business are one entity: the money the business makes is the money you make. You must report your income on your federal tax return. You will also need to fill out and attach a Schedule C form for your business activity. (Depending on the amount of your earnings and expenses, you may be able to fill out a Schedule C-EZ, a simplified version of the form.)

If you plan to use a name other than your own for your business, in most states you are required to register that name. This fictitious name is known as your DBA ("doing business as") name. Registering a DBA name is done through your county clerk's office or through your state government. The website of the U.S. Small Business Administration (http://www.sba.gov) provides information about the process. Of course, you'll want to think of a name that is memorable and gives customers a clear idea of your service or product.

Customers and Competition

Who are your intended customers? What competition will you have? These are important parts of your business plan. If you can't identify your potential customers, how are you going to get them to buy your work? If you're unaware of your competition, how do you know you can successfully compete? Your potential customers might include people who are buying birthday or holiday gifts, people who are decorating their home, people who are getting married, or people who have a new baby.

Your competition consists of the other companies that offer a similar product or service. For the ceramics business, your competition may be online. Your competition may also include department stores, gift shops, and other stores that offer the type of dishware you have in mind. Check out what they are selling. One advantage you have is that you're a local artist with unique goods. Chances are, your

Although many artists are out there who want to make money using their skills, don't be discouraged by the competition. Find a way to be different, and get the word out!

work will be different enough that these larger stores will not be competing directly with you.

Get the Word Out

Your plan should include your strategies for informing people about your business and generating sales. For example, you might contact local decorators to see if they are interested in custom work for their clients. You might prepare a flyer to be displayed in the offices or gift shops of local houses of worship. Asking the hospital gift shop to display your flyer might be a good way to reach new parents.

How many pieces do you plan to create each month? How confident are you that you can sell these pieces? These are important questions to consider. It might be a good idea to start out with a few confirmed orders in hand. In any case, you'll need more than a hunch, guess, or good feeling about

Having an online presence is key to succeeding. Regardless of what form your art takes, find a way to present it online so that customers can see your great skills!

how many customers you'll have. You'll need to have a plan in place to meet with or attract customers and a good reason to believe your plan is going to work.

Many people do an internet search for the services they need. Because of this, it's important to have a website and social media accounts. You can start with a free Facebook page and a blog for your business. Check out some keyword ranking sites and see which terms related to your product or service rank high in the search engines. Be sure to use those terms in your description of your business, as well as in your posts. Don't forget to include photos of your work. Invite friends and relatives to "like" your business page to help spread the word.

Budgeting

A budget is important for a new business enterprise. It should list all the items you will need to spend money on. For example, if you are making flyers you'll need to include paper; copying services or ink cartridges; tacks, staples, or adhesive putty; and any other necessary supplies. If you intend to print business cards, those costs should be included. If you plan to package items in special boxes or with a sticker that has your company's name on it, you need to include those costs, too. The fees for shipping or delivering products to customers are another key cost.

Some of your costs will be the same no matter how many customers you have. For instance, printing business cards is going to cost a certain amount no matter what. Other costs are going to depend on how many pieces you produce or customers you have. For instance, each ceramic piece will have a cost that includes studio time and materials. The more pieces you make, the higher the cost. Separate your budget into two parts. One will have the costs that don't vary. These are known as fixed costs. The other will have the costs that do vary. These are known as variable costs.

Price Point and Profit

Your price point is a vital piece of your business plan. If your work is priced too high, you may not generate enough sales volume to cover all of your costs. If your work is priced too low, you may have a large number of orders but lose money on each one. That's why it's important to determine the profit you will make on each piece.

The profit is the amount of money you make after all of your costs are covered. Let's say a large bowl costs you $25 to make. That amount includes the cost of materials and the fee for the time at the ceramics shop. If you sell the bowl for $25, you cover your costs for the bowl, but you make no money for

CUSTOMER SATISFACTION

It's easier to keep a customer than it is to find a new one. You want customers to come back and tell their friends and relatives about you. Keeping people happy isn't difficult if you plan and put everything in a signed agreement.

The most important step is for everyone to agree on what the finished product should look like before you begin. As an artist, you'll need to sketch a preliminary design. Get the customer's signature on the sketch to show approval of the design. Include samples of the colors and materials you have in mind. If you want to change something along the way, make sure everyone agrees on the change.

Make sure milestone dates and customer expectations (like availability for a clothing fitting) are established in your agreement. Treat customers the way you would like to be treated and deliver the agreed-upon product on time.

your labor. You also have no money to help pay for the flyers you made to advertise your business or any other start-up costs.

As the business owner, you need to decide how much more than $25 to charge. One way of doing that is to take all your general business costs (other than the costs of making the piece) and divide them by the number of pieces you plan to sell. By taking this overhead and including it in the price for each piece, you will be sure you cover all your costs. You also need to include an amount that is your profit.

When all is said and done, it's possible that a bowl that costs you $25 to make will sell for $40 or more. If you set the price at $40, you will make $15 on each bowl. Of course, not all of that is yours to keep. Part of that amount will go to cover your business costs. After all your costs are covered, the money that remains will be pure profit.

When starting and running a business, understanding costs and profits is critical. If you need help understanding the financial parts of business, ask a business or math teacher for help.

To decide how much to charge, it can be helpful to look at how much money you are investing to start your business. For instance, if you are investing $500, you will spend some of that amount on marketing and office supplies. Some will go toward making any samples you want to have on hand. That money will also pay for your portfolio. If you know you want to make back the $500 you've already spent, cover the cost of the items you'll create for your customers, and have a bit of money that is profit, you're well on the way to coming up with a selling price that will work for your business.

Be aware that when doing custom work, you can ask your customers for a deposit at the start of a project. This can help you cover the cost of art supplies. For example, you can ask for 50 percent in the beginning and 50 percent at the end.

Keep a Record

A big part of running a business is keeping track of information. You need to be diligent about tracking all of the money coming in and money going out. You also need to keep track of your clients and projects you're working on.

The simplest way to track your first customers is to create a record for each customer. It could be an index card with all the information about that customer and that project. It could be a record in a database application or a row in a spreadsheet. Use whatever makes the most sense to you.

Keep copies of your client agreements in a notebook, paper file, or computer folder where you can get to them easily. Use a calendar to track when any money is due to you. Make a note in green so you know it's about money coming in. If someone is more than a week late in paying you, politely call or email to remind him or her.

Keep a copy of any invoices you need to pay. Store them using the same method you use for your client agreements. Mark your calendar in red to remind yourself of payments that must be mailed by a certain date to reach your vendors in time.

All of this information will help you in keeping your business running smoothly. It will also be important when it is time to pay income taxes. Ask an adult with experience to help you the first time you have taxes to pay. If you can't find anyone, at tax time there are often volunteers at the local library who can help you out.

Succeeding

There's no better way to get your foot in the door than gaining experience. However, simply getting experience isn't the final result you're looking for. You want to succeed as a small business owner or as an employee for a company that's hired you for your skills. Between your first forays into the

Never let the business aspects of making money as an artist make you forget your true goal: to be a successful artist. Continue honing your skills by doing what you love.

working world and your dream career is a transition you have to take control of.

No one in this world is more interested in your success than you, and no one else knows the ins and outs of what you like and don't like. You're also the only one who can truly say which environments and job responsibilities you're comfortable with and interested in. Now that you've got some experience under your belt, it's time to leverage that to find a job, get admitted into college or a specialized program, or start your own business.

Let's Get Started

You may think you'll remember the details of all your volunteer positions or part-time jobs. But it is easy to forget. The best thing to do is to create an index card, computer file, or notebook page with the details of each job. Do this as soon as your job is finished, if not before. Include your responsibilities, how long the project took, and the key people you worked with. Record the contact information for the supervisor to whom you reported. If you have a letter of recommendation from a project or job, keep it in the file or notebook with the rest of the information about it. Be sure to take photos of the finished work, too, and keep it with the other materials.

No matter what you do along your voyage toward becoming a successful artist, keep a record! File away contact information of people you've worked with and details of every job you do.

While you are working at a position, remember to ask if you can use your supervisor as a reference. Also take any opportunity to talk about possible career options with each employer. Your supervisors may know about types of jobs that are new to you. These jobs may use your artistic talents in ways that fit you perfectly. They also may know of interesting

summer or university programs that will help you launch your career. You won't know unless you politely ask for a bit of their time and tell them about what you hope to accomplish in the art field.

In the arts, your portfolio is vital to your success. You may include different items, depending on the opportunity, but be sure to include samples of your work that showcase your abilities and creativity. The items you include should give a good idea of who you are as an artist. Your portfolio should also include a summary of your experience, letters of recommendation, and references.

Academic Applications

Just the thought of writing an essay for admission to an academic program is enough to make most of us sweat. It needs to be well written and organized. It needs to be impressive. It needs to be succinct. It needs to be brilliant.

In truth, the admission essay is an excellent opportunity to turn your experience into success. In many cases, applicants are asked to write several essays. Make sure one of your essays is about the things you've learned as you've gained experience in the arts field. Describe the steps you've taken to find jobs and experiences that draw upon your

If you've taken steps in your artistic career by the time you apply for college, your college application and admissions letter are great opportunities to highlight your real-world experience.

artistic talents. Talk about the challenging and rewarding parts of those experiences. Discuss what you've gained as a result of your determination and creativity. Above all, be sure your essay highlights your experience while giving the admissions officers a sense of who you are.

NETWORK

You might have heard about networking. It can involve talking at formal interviews or meeting people for lunch. Networking is a great way to turn experience into success, especially for young people who are just starting out.

Networking can involve online professional networks, but it isn't just about social media. It is about speaking with people who can help you or who can introduce you to others who can help you. Perhaps there is a successful, small, and local business in your town. It may not have anything to do with art, but it has happy customers. Ask the owner if you can take her to lunch to inquire about her biggest challenges, how she attracts customers, and what she wishes she'd known before she started her business. You can learn a great deal from others who have blazed trails ahead of you.

The Job Search

Whether or not college is in your plans, you'll likely want to turn your experience into a paying job. The most important tools for landing a job are your portfolio and résumé, which should include a summary of your skills and experience. Be sure to include all of the significant work you've done, including experience you gained on your own. Include the length of time you worked at each position and your key achievements.

The interviewer will use your résumé to ask about your experience. Find a way to emphasize the experience that is most relevant to the artistic

At some point in your professional career as an artist, you'll look for and interview for jobs. Be ready with your portfolio and to speak confidently about your experience.

position you are seeking. Be polite, but don't be shy. An interview is one of your biggest chances to communicate positive information about yourself.

Don't be surprised if the interviewer asks you about your biggest mistakes or regrets. It's OK to admit that you have made errors. Keep the discussion light, and explain the way you fixed the situation or what you learned from it. The main point is to show that you've grown as a result of a negative experience.

If the questions you're asked don't provide the opportunity for you to stress your artistic talents and experience, stay calm. At the end of the interview, say that you'd like to mention your reasons for applying for the job. Take that opportunity to speak briefly about your talents, your experience, and the role you hope to play at the company.

Learn More

You're young. You're serious about starting and running your own business. You've read every book and article you can find. What other ways are there for you to learn more before you start your business?

Does your school have a club for aspiring entrepreneurs? Does it have a Junior Achievement program? If so, these could be good ways for you to

Youth-oriented groups in fields like business and art can help you as a young entrepreneur by providing support, valuable information, networking, and serve as a career launchpad.

get information and support as you plan and launch your business. If there isn't a club for entrepreneurial teens, now might be the perfect time to start one. Be sure to invite professionals from organizations involved in the arts to speak at the club.

Youth groups such as 4-H and scouting offer programs of interest to those starting businesses.

For instance, 4-H offers a curriculum in entrepreneurship. The Boy Scouts of America offers merit badges in entrepreneurship and salesmanship. Girl Scouts of the USA has a number of business-oriented badges, too. Local chambers of commerce and local arts guilds may offer support to entrepreneurial teens as well.

The U.S. Small Business Administration (SBA) offers helpful information for teens. A number of magazines focus on entrepreneurs and small businesses. Although most of their readers are adults, the advice and information they print applies to any small business owner. That includes you!

GLOSSARY

budget A plan for expenditures and income for a period of time.

business An enterprise that is started with the intention of making a profit.

business plan A plan for business success that includes costs, competition, estimates of sales activity, marketing strategies, and other important details.

client A person or organization who uses the services of a professional or company.

curator A person who manages or oversees the collections of a museum, art gallery, or similar institution.

customer A person or organization who buys the products from a business.

entrepreneur A person who starts and runs a business of his or her own.

hobby An activity a person engages in for enjoyment or relaxation.

initial investment The amount of money that is needed to start a business.

internship A temporary job placement that allows a person to get hands-on experience in a career field. An internship can be paid or unpaid.

investor A person or organization that contributes money to an endeavor, such as a business, with the expectation of getting a profit in return.

invoice A statement listing the goods delivered or services provided and the amount due for them; a bill.

licensing A contractual agreement that gives one or more companies permission to produce and sell products incorporating the design, artwork, or logo of another company.

limited liability company (LLC) A business structure available in most states that protects its owners from personal responsibility for company debts that exceed the amount the owners have invested.

marketing The action of promoting and selling products or services.

niche A specialized but profitable section of the market.

partner A person or organization that puts money into an endeavor with the expectation of receiving part of the potential profits.

pitch A line of talk designed to persuade.

profit The financial gain, especially the difference between the amount earned and the amount spent to produce the product.

reference A person who is in a position to speak

about a candidate's qualifications for a job and has agreed to do so.

revenue The income earned from a company's sales of products or services to its customers.

sales volume The quantity of total sales in a given period.

schedule C The federal tax form used to report business income or business losses for a sole proprietor, independent contractor, or self-employed individual.

sole proprietorship An unincorporated business with one owner who pays personal income tax on profits from the business.

transferable skills Abilities and personal qualities a worker can use in more than one occupation.

vendor A person or company that provides goods and services to a business; a supplier.

FURTHER READING

Books

Brown Hamilton, Tracy. *Cool Careers Without College for People Who Love the Arts*. New York, NY: Rosen Publishing, 2017.

Cuban, Mark, Ian McCue, and Shaan Patel. *Kid Start-Up: How You Can Be An Entrepreneur*. New York, NY: Diversion Books, 2018.

Martin, Steve. *Entrepreneur Academy*. London, UK: Ivy Kids, 2018.

Mooney, Carla. *Using Computer Science in Online Retail Careers*. New York, NY: Rosen Publishing, 2018.

Owen, Ruth. *I Can Start a Business!* New York, NY: Rosen Publishing, 2018.

Small, Cathleen. *Diversity in Business*. New York, NY: Rosen Publishing, 2019.

Sutherland, Adam. *Be A Young Entrepreneur*. London, UK: Wayland Publishers, 2018.

Websites

CareerAddict
Careeraddict.com
Find career advice, career testing, resume writing help, and job search assistance for young people and professionals.

Digital.com
digital.com/blog/young-entrepreneurs
This site offers mentorship and thorough help for
    starting and growing a successful business for
    young entrepreneurs.

Entrepreneur
Entrepreneur.com
This site offers advice for starting a business at
    every level.

BIBLIOGRAPHY

Abrams, Rhonda M. *The Successful Business Plan: Secrets & Strategies.* Palo Alto, CA: Planning Shop, 2003.

Bolles, Richard Nelson. *What Color Is Your Parachute? A Practical Manual for Job-Hunters and Career-Changers.* Berkeley, CA: Ten Speed Press, 2011.

Boy Scouts of America. "Introduction to Merit Badges." Retrieved April 2, 2019. www.scouting. org/meritbadges.aspx.

Bygrave, William D., and Andrew Zacharakis. *Entrepreneurship.* 2nd ed. Hoboken, NJ: Wiley, 2011.

CBS News. "Meet the teenage king of bow ties who just inked an NBA deal." July 7, 2017. www. cbsnews.com/news/mos-bows-bow-tie-empire -founder-signs-nba-deal/.

Christen, Carol, Richard Nelson Bolles, and Jean M. Blomquist. *What Color Is Your Parachute? For Teens: Discovering Yourself, Defining Your Future.* 2nd ed. Berkeley, CA: Ten Speed Press, 2010.

DeBaise, Colleen. *The Wall Street Journal Complete Small Business Guidebook.* New York, NY: Three Rivers Press, 2009.

Everett, Robert F. *The Entrepreneur's Guide to Marketing.* Westport, CT: Praeger, 2009.

Ewing Marion Kauffman Foundation. "Entrepreneurship." Retrieved April 2, 2019. www.kauffman.org/what-we-do/entrepreneurship.

Greene, Cynthia L. *Entrepreneurship* (21st Century Business). Mason, OH: South-Western Cengage Learning, 2011.

Hiser, Kevin. "Why Your Business Plan Is Probably Incomplete." Entrepreneur.com, August 20, 2012. Retrieved April 2, 2019. www.entrepreneur.com/article/224195.

Holzner, Steven. *Small Business Web Sites Made Easy.* New York, NY: McGraw-Hill, 2009.

Levinson, Jay Conrad, Jeannie Levinson, and Amy Levinson. *Guerrilla Marketing: Easy and Inexpensive Strategies for Making Big Profits from Your Small Business.* 4th ed. Boston, MA: Houghton Mifflin, 2007.

McKeever, Mike P. *How to Write a Business Plan.* 9th ed. Berkeley, CA: Nolo, 2008.

National 4-H Cooperative Curriculum System, Inc. "Entrepreneurship." Retrieved April 2, 2019. https://4-h.org/parents/curriculum/entrepreneurship/.

National Service-Learning Clearinghouse. "Youth Topics." Retrieved April 2, 2019. https://youth.gov/youth-topics.

Perry, Elle. "Memphis 'kidpreneur' Mo's Bows takes stock and looks to 2018." *Memphis Business Journal*, January 3, 2018. www.bizjournals.com /memphis/news/2018/01/03/memphis-kidpreneur -mos-bows-takes-stock-and-looks.html

Phillpott, Siôn. "The 9 Most Successful Teen Entrepreneurs in the World (2018)." CareerAddict.com, November 14, 2018. www.careeraddict.com/teen-entrepreneurs.

Porter, Jane. "How to Build Credibility as a Young Entrepreneur." Entrepreneur.com, August 8, 2011. Retrieved April 2, 2019. www.entrepreneur.com/article/220119.

Scarborough, Norman M., Doug Wilson, and Thomas Zimmerer. *Essentials of Entrepreneurship and Small Business Management*. 6th ed. Upper Saddle River, NJ: Prentice Hall, 2011.

Stephenson, James, and Courtney Thurman. *Ultimate Small Business Marketing Guide: 1500 Great Marketing Tricks That Will Drive Your Business Through the Roof*. 2nd ed. Irvine, CA: Entrepreneur Press, 2007.

U.S. Department of Labor. "I Am 18." Youth Rules. Retrieved April 2, 2019. www.youthrules.dol. gov/know-the-limits/18.htm.

U.S. Department of Labor. "I Am 14 or 15." Youth Rules. Retrieved April 2, 2019. www.youthrules. dol.gov/know-the-limits/14-15.htm.

U.S. Department of Labor. "I Am 16 or 17." Youth Rules. Retrieved April 2, 2019. www.youthrules. dol.gov/know-the-limits/16-17.htm.

U.S. Department of Labor, Wage and Hour Division. "Child Labor Provisions for Nonagricultural Occupations Under the Fair Labor Standards Act (FLSA)." Retrieved April 2, 2019. www.dol.gov/whd/regs/compliance /childlabor101.htm.

U.S. Small Business Administration. "Create Your Business Plan." Retrieved April 2, 2019. www. sba.gov/starting-business/write-your-business -plan%20.

INDEX